AN ALBUM OF NAZISM

AN ALBUM OF NAZISM

WILLIAM LOREN KATZ

FRANKLIN WATTS ■ NEW YORK ■ LONDON ■ 1979

To Ernie, Erika, Naomi, Phyllis, Patty, Barbara,
Howie, Warren, Thorne, Virginia, Jack, and Al.

Acknowledgments
The author and the publisher would like to express
their appreciation to the American Jewish Committee
for their help in locating photographs for this book.
Additicnal gratitude is expressed to the Anti-Defamation
League of B'nai B'rith for a special research grant.

Cover design by Ginger Giles
Cover photographs courtesy of:
Library of Congress: left and center.
Anti-Defamation League: right.

Photographs courtesy of:
U.S. Army: opp. p. 1; American Jewish Committee: pp. 3
(top and bottom), 32, 34, 38 (center), 44, 51 (top right),
55 (right), 66, 68, 69, 73, 74 (top right and bottom), 76, 77,
78, 80, 81, 82, 85 (bottom), 86 (right); Naomi Warnov: p.
3 (center); Library of Congress: pp. 4, 6, 7, 8, 10, 14 (top
right), 17, 18 (bottom), 21, 22, 24, 25 (top), 27, 30, 31, 35,
37, 38 (top), 41, 42, 43, 47 (bottom), 51 (bottom), 52, 55
(left), 56, 58, 59, 60, 63, 72, 74 (top left); National Archives:
p. 28 (bottom); N.A./W.W. II Coll. of Seized Enemy Records:
pp. 11, 25 (bottom), 38 (bottom), 47 (top), 48, 51 (top
left), 61; N.A./Signal Corps.: p. 14 (top left and bottom);
N.A./U.S. Information Agency: pp. 28 (top), 62; Catherine
Noren: pp. 13, 70, 71; Institute of Contemporary History
and Wiener Library: p. 18 (top); French Embassy Press and
Information Division: p. 65; Author's collection: p. 85 (top
left); Anti-Defamation League: pp. 85 (top right), 86 (left).

Library of Congress Cataloging in Publication Data

Katz, William Loren.
An album of nazism.

Bibliography: p.
Includes index.
SUMMARY: Photographs and text describe
German nazism of the 1930's and 40's and
highlight the Nazi movement world-wide today.
1. Germany—History—1933–1945—Juvenile literature.
2. National socialism—History—Juvenile literature.
3. Fascism—Germany, West—Juvenile literature.
4. Fascism—United States—Juvenile literature.
[1. Germany—History—1933–1945. 2. National
socialism—History. 3. Fascism—History] I. Title.
DD256.5.K29   943.086   78–12723
ISBN 0–531–01500–9

CONTENTS

**Nazism goose-stepped
its way over all of Europe
during World War II.**

Can you imagine a dictatorship so cruel and powerful it

- controlled the right of its citizens to read, see, hear, and do what they wished;
- put to death millions of people for their religion, race, or politics;
- unleashed mankind's most destructive war to gain world domination;
- waged war against civilians, prisoners, men, women, and children;
- almost conquered the world?

Unthinkable? Unreal? Impossible?

No—unfortunately it all happened. In the middle of this century in Germany, a force called nazism grew, gained power, and brought on World War II.

Together with Italy and Japan, Nazi Germany almost dominated the world by 1942. Only the unity of the nations of the world, Communist and democratic, crushed its plan. But it could all happen again.

There are people today in Europe and America proud to call themselves Nazis. They are organized, have money, and issue propaganda. Sometimes they venture into the streets, hold rallies, or challenge those whom they hate. Even the defeated Nazis of World War II are stirring again in Germany.

Because nazism was once a powerful force and because it is again on the move, we need to know about it. The last time, people did not understand it until it was too late.

NAZISM YESTERDAY AND TODAY

FROM HIGH TIDE TO EBB TIDE

On the threshold of world domination by the middle of World War II, nazism was finally defeated. Today it no longer rules any nation, though its ideas are still alive and its followers growing.

In South America, Asia, South Africa, Europe, and North America, nazism lives on. Young men again don Nazi uniforms, armbands, and helmets—and march into demonstrations looking for trouble. On pleasant tree-lined streets on all continents, Nazi war criminals live out peaceful lives. In Germany, storm trooper units meet to recall the good old days and plan glorious new ones.

A LIVE ISSUE

Today nazism is very much a live issue. Men and women in the Netherlands, Italy, and the United States have been arrested as Nazi war criminals. In New York City the Board of Education introduced a course on the holocaust—the Nazi murder of six million Jews. The president of the German-American Committee of Greater New York protested by saying, "There is no real proof that the holocaust actually happened." In Skokie, Illinois, the American Nazi party planned a march into a Jewish area under the banner "Six Million More." They paraded in St. Louis and Chicago. These events took place in 1978.

It all happened before—the marches, the holocaust, the threats to minorities. Many have forgotten, and others never learned about it. For a long time, many texts described nazism simply as a wartime foe of the United States led by a dictator named Adolf Hitler. But nazism was more than that. It was the most total dictatorship to rule a major nation. It was a threat to world peace and freedom. It brought untold suffering and left an ugly scar on world history. And it is not yet dead.

Above: in 1963, members of the U.S. Nazi party were arrested for rioting. Middle: in 1977 Americans demonstrated against the American Nazi party and the KKK. Right: tombstones in a Jewish cemetery in America were smeared with swastikas in the 1970s.

Above: German radicals repeatedly demonstrated before the Reichstag after World War I. Right: during the Great Depression, wealthy bankers and businessmen aided the Nazi party, their funds paying for its march to power.

WHAT IS NAZISM?

THE NAZI IDEA

Nazism was not a new philosophy but an old set of ideas, fears, and hatreds. Through a false history and twisted science, it beat the drum for dictatorship, imperialism, and war. It claimed that Germans were destined to rule the world.

Minorities, Nazis argued, deserved enslavement or death. Nazism detested communism for its strength, and democracy for its weakness. War built man's virtues while peace, representative government, and religion sapped his power.

Nazism paraded as a "patriotic anti-communism" to "save the nation." Actually, it sought a ruthless dictator to control the lives of each citizen, to determine what each would hear, see, read, think, and do. Each owed the state absolute obedience, and those who disagreed were destroyed.

These ideas would lead to genocide and a more terrifying war than the world had ever seen.

DER FÜHRER

In a time of economic and political collapse, Nazis called for a dictator to act as the "Leader"—*der Führer*—of the nation. (In Italy, Mussolini was also called the Leader—il Duce.) People longed for a hero to lead them out of misery and uncertainty, and away from the threat of communism.

The price of der Führer was military control of the nation and totalitarian power. There was no appeal from his decisions. To lead the nation from chaos to glory, all must march to his step.

THE MAIN SUPPORT

The leading backers of the Nazi party were Germany's industrialists and bankers. Fearful of communism and the unions, they supported men who promised, through a dictatorship, to protect their mills, mines, and investments.

As Germany marched toward world war, these men saw new possibilities for land, profit, and expansion. This, not Germany, was their interest. They reaped the reward of more armaments, use of slave workers, and seizure of new territories. They financed Hitler, the Nazis, and World War II.

THE BASIC BELIEFS OF NAZISM

THE UNYIELDING INGREDIENTS

The leading ideas that powered nazism have been around for a long time. They were not invented by Nazis, only honed to a fine point and given some strange or extreme twists.

EXTREME NATIONALISM OR CHAUVINISM

Nazis distorted the normal love of country into a hatred for other nations. Patriotism became fanaticism, and people were taught to follow the will of their government and be ready to die for their country. This chauvinism escalated into a desire to seize other countries and wage war against innocent people.

RACISM

Racism was hardly new to the world. Hatred of minorities surfaced in every country of the world. In the United States the Ku Klux Klan (KKK) for decades carried on campaigns against blacks, Catholics, Jews, foreigners, and union organizers. Nazis took the traditional hatred of Jews and drove it to the point of mass murder. During World War II they also began massacres of Gypsies, Russians, Poles, and other *Untermenschen,* or "inferior people."

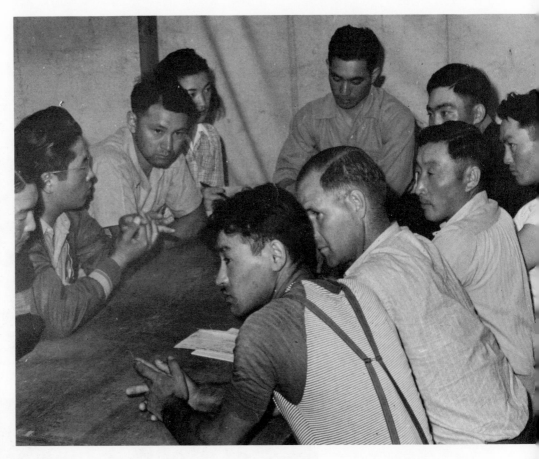

Opposite: racism dominated the KKK in America as well as the Nazi party in Germany. Right: concentration camps appeared not only in Germany but were also used to confine Japanese-Americans in the United States during World War II.

MILITARY DICTATORSHIP Adolf Hitler was not the first dictator, nor the first to establish a military state. Throughout recorded history, rulers have demanded obedience and invaded, seized, or destroyed foreign nations. The training of a nation's youth for war has been a common way of threatening opposition at home and uniting a people behind a dictator.

Nazi rule meant absolute power over citizens, over what they could see, hear, think, and do. Police, spies, and midnight raids kept the population afraid to speak out. To fail to march in step to Nazi rule often meant disappearing from sight.

IMPERIALISM The lust for overseas colonies helped spark World War I. The Nazis made imperialism a main policy, and warfare its leading method. They sought to rule the world and lift Germany out of the Great Depression by invading and using the resources of others.

Above: guarded by police, Germans line up for coal and bread. Right: showing the desperation of the time, the poor of Berlin ransack the debris after market day.

THE FASCIST BUILDUP POSES AS ANTI-COMMUNISM

RISE OF WORLD COMMUNISM If there had been no communism after World War I, there would have been no rise of fascism or nazism. Nazism was one dangerous, deadly, calculated reaction to the victories of communism. Communism meant state control of property and business.

In 1917 Communist-led workers and soldiers seized power in Russia. The Communist state abolished private property and called on European workers to overthrow capitalism, or free enterprise. In 1918 in Germany, workers, soldiers, and sailors tried to seize power in Kiel, Bavaria, and Berlin. In 1919 Austrian workers stormed Parliament, but were beaten back by a volunteer army. In Hungary, Communists won power, but were overthrown. In Italy, workers in the north seized factories and peasants in the south seized farming land. They were eventually ousted.

The Communist threat then faded. It retreated back within the borders of the Soviet Union. But one of the forces to beat it back —world fascism—stood ready to take power itself.

RISE OF WORLD FASCISM The hysteria generated by the rise of communism panicked the rich and middle classes. They wanted to protect private property, their jobs, and their homes. The wealthy were determined to protect their investments, lands, and factories. To combat communism, they turned toward angry, bitter, and often violent ex-soldiers who fought Communists in the streets. This strange alliance of the well-to-do and criminal veterans became the movement called fascism or nazism.

In Germany these veterans were called the "Free Corps." Later these gangs joined the "Brownshirts" of the Nazi party. They roamed the streets attacking Communists, liberals, and those who did not agree with their definition of patriotism.

In Italy these veterans were called "Blackshirts" and organized in the Fascist party by Benito Mussolini. In one five-month period they destroyed 120 union headquarters, invaded 200 Socialist offices, killed 243 people, and wounded another 1,444. In 1922 they marched on Rome with Mussolini, who was appointed dictator by King Victor Emmanuel.

By then it should have been clear that fascism and nazism posed a threat to nations greater than communism. But governments remained more worried about communism, and deaf to cries that nazism had become the leading threat to law and order.

Opposite: ushered in by Benito Mussolini, fascism came to Italy. The Italian and German dictators admired each other and formed an alliance. Below: during an early rally, Hitler waves to a crowd.

THE FERTILE SOIL OF AUTHORITARIAN GERMANY

THE PRUSSIAN TRADITION

If nazism was born anywhere in particular, it was probably in the soil of Prussia, a province in northern Germany. Prussia was ruled by *Junkers,* or landed aristocrats who admired warfare, hated democracy, and believed in dictatorship. The Junkers sought an authoritarian state that would crush dissent, unions, and minorities and lead Germany toward glorious battles for new land.

Prussian Chancellor Otto von Bismarck devoted his life to unifying Germany through "blood and iron." He provoked and won wars against Denmark, Austria, and France. In 1871 he proclaimed the German Empire and crowned William I its Emperor, or Kaiser. The Kaisers followed in the arrogant, warlike Prussian tradition.

Because it arrived late on the scene of nations, Germany had few overseas colonies. Its bankers and industrialists demanded new lands to exploit, even if it meant taking them from Britain, France, and other European nations. Kaiser William II promised German armed forces would teach the world a few lessons.

WORLD WAR I

To prove its military prowess and gain new colonies, Kaiser William II led Germany into war in 1914. Expecting to overwhelm their enemies, German soldiers confidently marched off to war. After a four-year bloodbath, Germany was defeated and disgraced.

The war was a disaster for the world. Almost ten million soldiers and more than twenty million civilians lost their lives. The war cost a vast sum of money. In shattered lives it cost even more.

Germany also paid for defeat in new bitterness and hatred. Learning little from its loss, Germany blamed others. "The German army was stabbed in the back!" claimed Field Marshal von Hindenburg. Germans commonly blamed pacifists, Communists, liberals, Jews, and war profiteers—but not themselves. This lie and bitter legacy would lead only to another, worse war.

Military service
and war were part
of the German code
by World War I.

Below, left: the Treaty of Versailles humiliated Germany and brought a furious nationalism in response. Nazis would play on this anger. Right: this meeting assailed the Treaty of Versailles as unjust to Germans. Bottom: the German delegation to Versailles, shown here, bore the brunt of the national fury over the treaty.

POSTWAR GERMANY FIGHTS FOR SURVIVAL

The war left Germany in turmoil. The Kaiser fled and no one seemed to rule. People rioted for bread and coal. Soldiers, sailors, and workers seized power in Russia and established a Communist government. In Germany, similar groups tried to take over the government. Battles between Communists and anti-Communists raged in the town and countryside.

THE WEIMAR GOVERNMENT When William II fled, a weak government named after the town of Weimar, where it was formed, took over. It was run by conservative Socialists and backed by the German Army. It tried to suppress communism and halt the violence engulfing the nation.

Germans had no experience of representative government, and many did not want democracy. Its people, ruled by aristocrats and military leaders, were trained to obey orders. Since the Weimar government believed the greatest threat came from communism, it repeatedly allowed anti-Communists to break the law.

In a desperate situation, this made matters worse. Streets became public forums and then battlegrounds. The Allied food blockade of Germany, which continued into 1919, caused starvation. Frightened men argued and fought over the future of Germany. The Free Corps smashed Communist and Socialist meetings, toppled speakers, and invaded opposition newspapers.

THE TREATY OF VERSAILLES To add to their misery, Germans were forced to accept the humiliating Treaty of Versailles. The victorious Allies made Germany accept full war guilt and pay reparations to its old enemies. Germany was stripped of its colonies, and some of its land was given to France. Its army was cut down to 100,000 volunteers, its navy reduced to a few ships, and its air force disbanded.

For a military nation, this was too much to bear. Anger fueled misery and exploded in violence. The German Chancellor who was asked to sign the treaty refused, saying, "May the hand wither that signs this treaty!"

DEFEAT OF THE LEFT, RISE OF THE RIGHT

POLITICS WITH GUNS

A wave of assassinations followed in the wake of the treaty. From 1918 to 1922, 376 citizens were slain for political reasons.

Most of the murders—354—were committed by right-wing or conservative assassins. But the Weimar government moved only against the left-wing or pro-Communists. Of the ten assassins condemned to death for murder, all were from the left wing. Each time, the government assumed that the only threat to law and order came from the left wing.

This injustice would be duly noted and played upon by a new group getting under way—the Nazis. Street violence was tolerable when conducted against liberals, Communists, pacifists, and others of the Left.

COMMUNIST PLANS FOILED

The Weimar government played out its role as defender of the state against the assaults of the Left. In some instances the German Army intervened, and in others the Free Corps beat back revolutionary efforts.

This strategy led to increased power for right-wingers, who had no more love of the government than left-wingers. In 1920 the Free Corps seized the Berlin government while the army watched. Only a workers' strike forced the return of the regular government.

From 1919 on, Communist power ebbed. It never reached more than 18 percent of the total vote. But the strength of anti-communism, enjoying official support, was on the rise.

THE NAZI PARTY IS BORN

In 1919 the army sent a decorated young veteran, Adolf Hitler, to investigate the German Workers' party. The military was seeking a political force to carry forth its own ideas. In this tiny group Hitler became the seventh member.

He also became its leading light and master organizer. By then his ideas had formed. He hated communism, democracy, Jews,

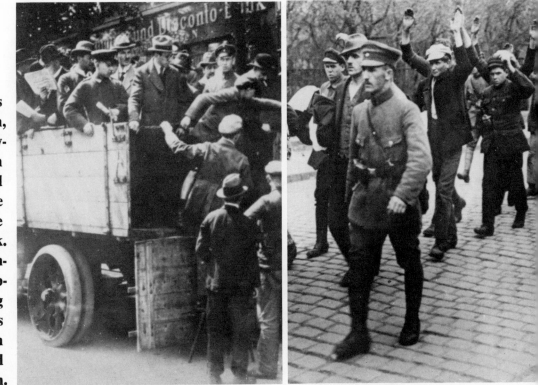

Right: strikes were common, and this trolley-bus strike in 1919 caused Berliners to hire trucks to take them to work. Far right: Communists captured during demonstrations at Eiserfeld in 1921 are led to prison.

liberals, and peace. For him war was "the greatest of all experiences." Germany should be ruled by a military dictator who would provide a war to raise national self-esteem and gain back Germany's colonies. He would be der Führer, or leader.

A brilliant speaker and politician, Hitler whipped the small group into a fighting unit. He changed its name to the National Socialist German Workers' party, helped write out its views for voters, designed its first flag, and picked the swastika as its emblem. The swastika first appeared in the Bronze Age and spread all over the world except among Egyptians and Semites.

THE NAZI APPEAL The party carefully designed its approach to win votes. It talked of socialism, which was popular among workers, and promised the middle class and the rich the protection of capitalism. Its talk of a new war that would create jobs and gain new land appealed to militarists and industrialists.

Right: housewives had to carry baskets of inflated marks to market. **Below, left:** the French seize coal in the Ruhr, adding cold homes to other German humiliations. **Below, right:** this German family in the Ruhr faced starvation.

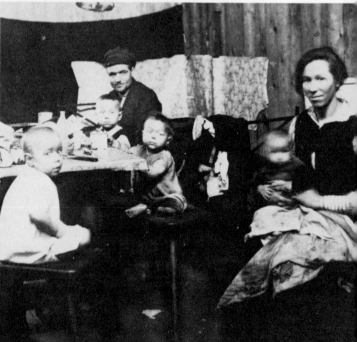

THE BEER HALL PUTSCH

RISING INFLATION AND UNEMPLOYMENT

Nazism was fed by worsening economic conditions, its star rising with soaring inflation and unemployment. In 1920 it took 60 to 80 German marks to buy a U.S. dollar. Three years later it took 7,000 marks. For German men and women this meant less food. And in 1923 unemployment reached six million in a population of sixty million.

When Germany could no longer pay its reparations, French troops rolled into the Ruhr valley and cut off four-fifths of Germany's coal, steel, and pig iron. National discontent rose, and angry, unemployed young men joined Nazi street gangs.

The Weimar government advocated passive resistance to the French, but Nazis whipped up fury toward the government, liberals, Jews, and the Treaty of Versailles. Now more people listened to their propaganda.

THE MUNICH PUTSCH

In 1923 the Nazis thought their time had come. A year before, Mussolini's Fascists, claiming they would save Italy from communism, had taken power. If Mussolini could use veterans to seize the government, so could Hitler and his Nazis.

During a meeting of Bavarian officials in a Munich beer hall, Nazi storm troopers burst into the hall and surrounded the building. Hitler leaped onto a table, fired a pistol, and announced, "The national revolution has begun!" He claimed (falsely) that the army barracks and police station were in Nazi hands. Then he left to settle matters elsewhere. That was a mistake. The Bavarian officials escaped and the putsch collapsed.

THE SECOND ATTEMPT

The next day the Nazis tried again, with General Ludendorff leading 3,000 storm troopers against the War Ministry. The police drew back, but in a narrow street confronted the marchers. Shots were fired, and 16 Nazis and 3 police fell dead.

Nazi leaders scattered. Hitler, injured in a fall, escaped in a waiting car. Only General Ludendorff marched proudly to the end of the street. Hitler was arrested and jailed, and the Nazi movement was shattered.

REBUILDING THE PARTY

CHANGES IN CONDITIONS

Instead of a death sentence for treason, Hitler served less than nine months in prison. His prison life was more like life in a country club, and he was able to write down his plans for Germany and the world in *Mein Kampf* (*My Struggle*). He told what was coming, but few paid any attention.

Upon his release, Hitler threw himself into reorganizing his party. But prosperity had returned, unemployment and inflation had faded, and American aid enabled Germany to pay reparations again. Few listened to the Nazi screech about a Red revolution. In 1928 the party had only 108,000 members, polled less than 3 percent of the total vote, and elected 12 out of 490 Reichstag deputies. It was the ninth and weakest party in the national legislature.

If prosperity spelled doom for the Nazis, depression meant opportunity.

THE WORLD DEPRESSION

In 1929 the stock market crash in America triggered a world depression. From New York to Berlin, hungry men and women without jobs lined up for bread and soup, and their children cried for milk. U.S. aid to Germany halted, and again grim-faced Germans talked of revolution and a dictator to set things right.

In 1930 Nazi voting power increased seven times over, its deputies increased from 12 to 107 in the Reichstag, and it moved from ninth to second place among all parties. Nazi membership rose to 200,000, and more than half the members served in the street gangs that bloodied their foes.

German bankers and industrialists, fearful of communism and strikes, listened to Nazi claims to halt both. Leading millionaires began to finance nazism as a bulwark against communism, trade unions, and liberalism. Nazi talk of rebuilding the German Army and breaking the Treaty of Versailles sounded like a good investment.

Left: a determined Adolf Hitler leaves prison in
1924. Middle: a Nazi rally in 1928 drew thousands
of citizens. Right: a Republican rally in 1931
showed many anti-Nazis wearing military uniforms.

THE ELECTIONS OF 1932

Five times in 1932 Germans went to the polls, and five times Nazis failed to win a majority, capturing only a third of the vote. Storm troopers bloodied noses, dragged down speakers, and disrupted meetings, but the population vote did not swing firmly toward nazism.

By the year's end the Nazi vote had slipped and the Communist vote had risen. Cooperation between Socialists and Communists might have stopped nazism, but these two old rivals did not unite.

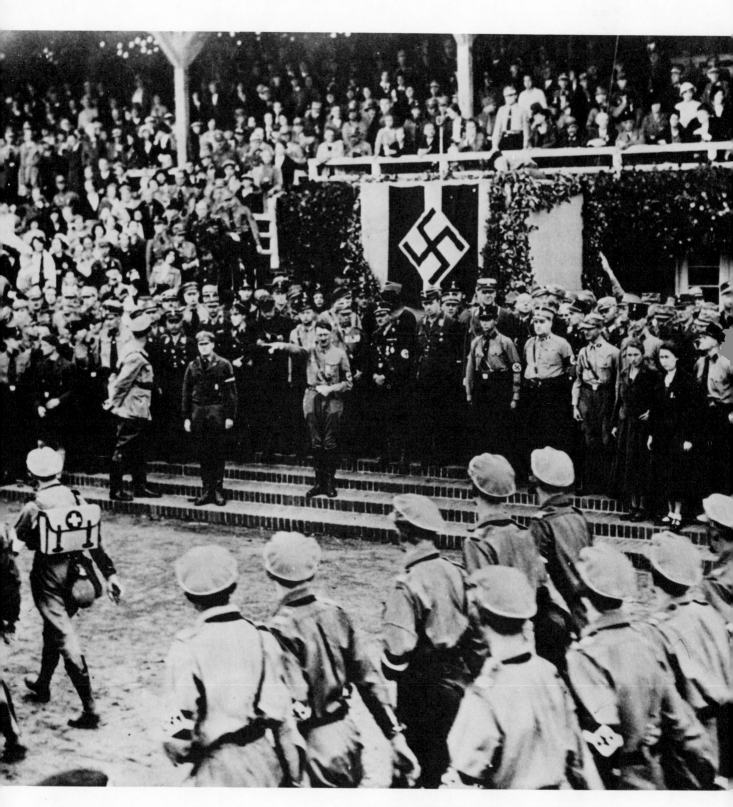

**In the midst of an election campaign,
Hitler salutes the Nazi youth in Potsdam.**

PROPAGANDA, VIOLENCE, AND THE MARCH TO POWER

THE SPEECHES OF 1932

Nazi propaganda campaigns were the envy of their foes. No other party made such dramatic use of torchlight rallies, loudspeakers, airplanes, searchlights, and marching storm troopers.

In masterful speeches, Nazi leaders employed such words as "smash" and "crush" to create a feeling of power and determination. During the Great Depression, this made people feel they could do something about their conditions by following nazism.

Nazi leaders found lies more effective than truths in winning support. Hitler said people "more readily fall victim to the big lie than the small lie." His contempt for people was clear:

The masses are receptive only to forceful expressions. . . . Faith is harder to shake than knowledge. Love is less subject to change than respect. Hatred is more lasting than dislike.

THE USE OF VIOLENCE

Violence appeared in more than Nazi speeches. Ernst Röhm commanded the SA, or storm troopers, and unleashed them during elections. They ripped down opposition posters, dragged speakers from platforms, and broke up meetings. Nazis believed that violence, while offending some, attracted many others. To the jobless, frustrated, or hungry, violence seemed to say, "At least the Nazis are doing something!"

By January 1932 Röhm had 400,000 armed men under his control. In Prussia alone in one three-week period they engaged in 461 street fights. They attacked, crippled, and sometimes murdered people. Nazi violence was tolerated by the timid, conservative Weimar government, which feared communism more.

Nazi violence provided another benefit for the party. Hitler was able to pose as a man of peace, unwilling to let the SA seize power. Many Germans began to believe the best way to halt the Nazis' violence was to elect them to office. So Nazis gained votes from those who hated and those who accepted their violence. This further split their opposition. People, above all, wanted an end to uncertainty in their lives.

Left: this 1933 Nazi election poster promises, "Away from Misery, Away from the Jews!" Nazi posters were designed by Hitler. Opposite, top: Nazi torchlight and night parades dazzled everyone—friend and foe.

Right: this Nazi election poster told Germans to break their chains by voting for the Nazi party. Opposite, bottom: Hitler made use of gestures and violent language.

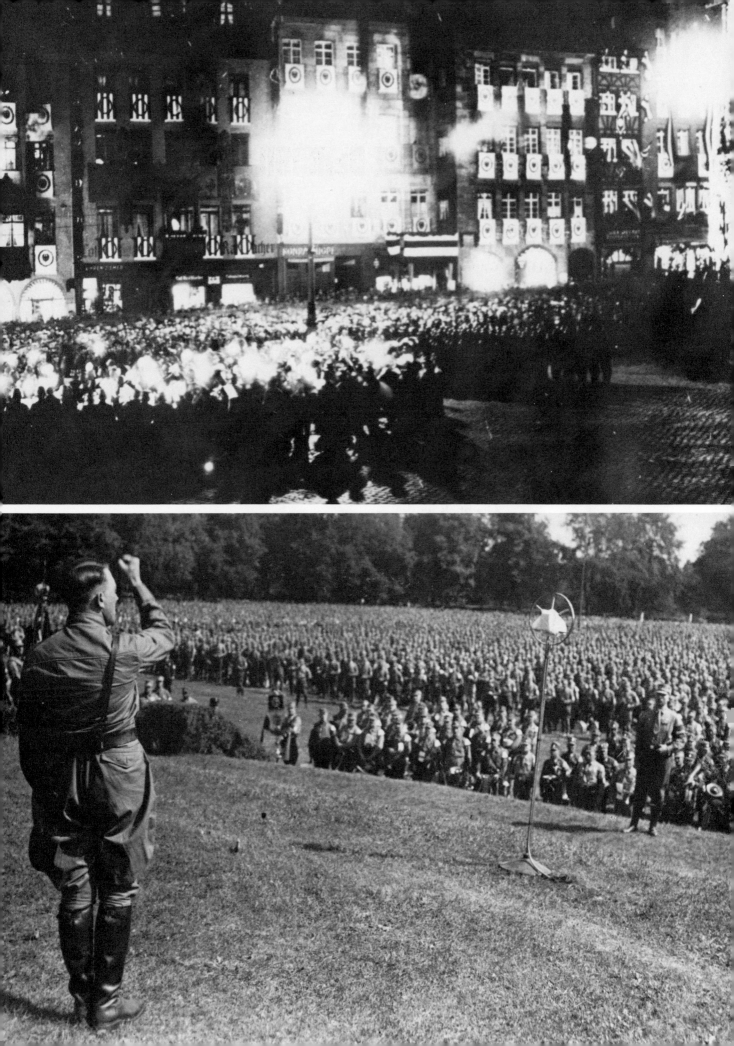

NAZISM ENTERS THE GERMAN GOVERNMENT

HITLER MADE CHANCELLOR

By the fifth election of 1932 that saw Nazi voting power slip and Communist strength gain, bankers, industrialists, militarists, and conservatives became worried. A series of back-room political deals had President Hindenburg appoint Hitler, whom he called the "vulgar little corporal," Chancellor of Germany on January 30, 1933. Hermann Göring became Prussian Minister of the Interior and Chief of Prussian Police.

Conservatives hoped this step would make Nazis respectable statesmen. Actually it opened the door to Nazi rule. The party began planning a new election that would give them a firm majority in the Reichstag. They would leave no possibility of their enemies winning.

As election day neared, Nazi propaganda expert Joseph Goebbels wrote:

Now it will be easy to carry on the fight, for we can call on all the resources of the state. Radio and press are at our disposal. We shall stage a master piece of propaganda. And this time, naturally, there is no lack of money.

THE MANIPULATED ELECTION

To ensure funds for victory, Hitler and Göring spoke before a secret meeting of industrialists and bankers. They promised to strangle unions, communism, and any threat of revolution. In simple words, they promised a dictatorship: "We stand before the last election." Germany's leading capitalists knew their contributions were purchasing the end of democratic government, and they gave fully to the Nazi campaign.

Propaganda and violence by Nazis had state support during the campaign. Opposition posters were torn down, speakers were afraid to address meetings, and newspaper offices were broken into and destroyed. Göring ordered his police to raid Communist headquarters and then announced, but never produced, proof of a "Red uprising."

President von Hindenburg was photographed with his appointee, Chancellor Adolf Hitler.

The nation was worked up to a fever pitch by Nazi arrests, charges, propaganda, and violence. Three days after the raid on Communist headquarters and seven days before the election, the Reichstag mysteriously burned to the ground. The Nazis charged the Communists with planning this "as a signal for a bloody insurrection."

The German voters went to the polls and gave the Nazis 44 percent of the vote. They were now within striking distance of total power.

Right: a dejected van der Lubbe sits in the courtroom. He claimed sole responsibility for the fire that altered German history, and was executed for his alleged part in it. Below, left: Communist leader in the Reichstag, Ernst Torgler speaks to the court that he claims has framed him and others. Below, right: Herman Göring testifies, offering evidence to prove Communists set the fire. His testimony was torn apart and ridiculed by Communist Georgi Dimitrov, and Göring stormed from the room.

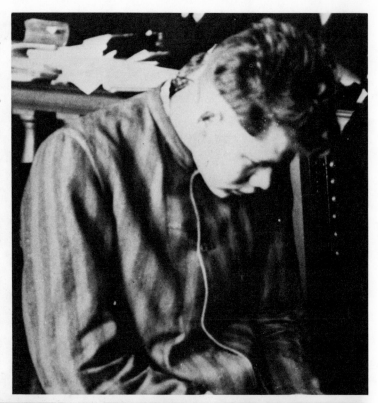

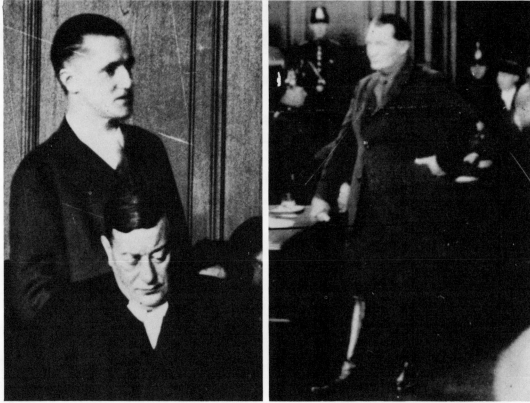

THE REICHSTAG FIRE AND TRIAL

"THE REICHSTAG IS ON FIRE!" The Reichstag fire, and the hysteria following it in the last week of the election, gave the Nazis that extra little push for votes. Yet the facts that came out after the election disprove their charge that it was a Communist plot.

During the fire, police arrested a Dutch youth, Marinus van der Lubbe, at the scene. He claimed to be a Communist and to have set the fire all by himself. Both claims are doubtful, and he was probably demented. He was the least important actor in the events that followed.

Claiming that the Communists were responsible for the fire, Göring ordered his police to seize suspects, and 4,000 Communists were arrested. Hitler had President Hindenburg sign an emergency decree allowing Nazis to limit freedom of speech, press, and assembly, to arrest and detain people, to open mails, and to enter homes without search warrants.

THE REICHSTAG FIRE TRIAL The trial of van der Lubbe and the Communists opened as storm troopers began a reign of terror in the country. They arrested and beat leading Communists, Socialists, and liberals—anyone they thought a threat to their rule.

Nazis invited the world press to the court. Each day the accused—van der Lubbe, Georgi Dimitrov, Ernst Torgler, Vassili Tanev, and Simon Popov—were brought in weighed down with painful and illegal chains. The Nazi judge ignored pleas for their removal. Bulgarian Communist George Dimitrov turned the trial against nazism. He claimed Nazis set the fire as part of a campaign of brutality, violence, and pressure to steal elections.

To refute Dimitrov, Göring and Goebbels testified, but Dimitrov courteously challenged their stories. Göring exploded at Dimitrov, "You wait till I get you out of the power of this court!" The world understood what Nazi justice meant.

Nazi evidence and witnesses were laughed at, and Nazi judges could convict only van der Lubbe, who was executed. Although the four Communists went free, Nazis would make sure no one would ever escape their "justice" again.

THE ESTABLISHMENT OF THE THIRD REICH

A LEGAL DICTATORSHIP

Nazi deputies in the Reichstag proposed an "Enabling Act." It granted Hitler power to draft a bill and have it become law in twenty-four hours—without Reichstag approval. As deputies gathered to vote, storm troopers surrounded the building and lined up in the corridors. Outside, Nazis shouted, "We want the bill—or fire and murder!"

Though the Nazis had only a minority of the deputies, the others surrendered to their pressure. Only 94 Socialists voted against the bill, and it passed with a vote of 441 for it.

The Nazis outside leaped to their feet, saluted, and shouted, "Heil Hitler!" Germany had become a dictatorship.

OUTLAWING THE OPPOSITION

The Nazis proclaimed a "New Order" and a "Thousand-Year Reich." The Communist party was outlawed, its leaders arrested and sent to concentration camps. Next Göring ordered police to seize buildings and funds owned by the Socialists. By mid-July all parties except the Nazis were outlawed.

At first Nazis did not attack religion, but pretended to be friendly. Hitler shakes hands with a representative of the Vatican.

By 1933, book-burning had spread to many German cities.

Nazi authority spread throughout Germany. Local governments and state legislatures were abolished, and a Gauleiter, or local leader appointed by the Nazis, was placed in charge of each region. Each official was required to swear loyalty to der Führer, Adolf Hitler.

On May Day, the traditional workers' holiday, Hitler addressed a Berlin rally celebrating work, unions, and their leaders. The next day storm troopers raided trade unions and sent their leaders to concentration camps. Thus the bankers and industrialists were repaid for their financial aid.

ENDING FREE EXPRESSION

On the night of May 10, 1933, a student torchlight parade paused before the University of Berlin, and young men threw 20,000 books into a bonfire. Germany was burning ideas that conflicted with its New Order.

"These flames," said Propaganda Minister Joseph Goebbels, "not only illuminate the final end of the old era; they also light up the new." Books by famous German, British, American, and other authors were banned from Nazi Germany.

This photograph of an early concentration camp
provides a glimpse of despair and terror. Prisoners were
largely political (not religious) enemies of the state.

SILENCING ENEMIES OF THE STATE

Within a month of taking power, Nazis were silencing any who dared to challenge their views. Murder by daylight or disappearance by night brought a political silence to Germany. In 1933 there were 2,000 assassinations. Any and all critics of the new government were rooted out and sent to concentration camps.

THE CONCENTRATION CAMPS

By August 1933 concentration camps had become a part of the German landscape. An estimated sixty-five camps held about 80,000 men, women, and children charged with acts of disloyalty to the Third Reich, as the new regime was called. Eight strands of barbed wire enclosed each prison. Rooftops were patrolled by machine gunners, and spotlights stabbed the night darkness. Prisoners ranged from Communists, union leaders, and college professors to those who gossiped about Nazi figures or were "politically unstable."

Camp inmates suffered physical abuse, and sometimes torture and death. Heads were shaved, and people were given little food. Suicide was common. Many guards forced bribes from inmates or their families. Some guards took pleasure in beating prominent judges, intellectuals, or leaders of an earlier Germany. Prisoners were held for as long as officials wanted, and released only through bribes.

THE FIRST STEPS AGAINST THE JEWS

With the Nazis in power, their campaigns against Jews did not decrease but escalated. In the first three months, Jews were banished from the civil service and the professions. Suddenly 30,000 heads of families—1,000 lawyers, 3,500 doctors, 3,000 musicians, and 20,000 merchants and artisans—were without jobs.

Jews were legally banned from public resorts, parks, and beaches. In July 3,000 Jewish Nuremberg storekeepers were arrested and paraded through the streets by laughing storm troopers. Some were kicked for moving too slowly. Townspeople cheered the spectacle. In Stuttgart 300 Jews, rounded up in the early morning, were forced to lick the street. Nazis and other citizens laughed.

These actions prepared Germany for greater barbarity. A generation was being trained to accept atrocities without objection, to follow the state no matter where it led. Violence was used to win acceptance of nazism.

Opposite: a Nazi sign warns, "The Jews are our misfortune!" Above: street assaults, such as this one on a Jewish student on May 23, 1933, stepped up after Nazis came to power. Right: public humiliation of Jews marked Nazi tactics. This Munich Jew is forced to carry a sign saying, "I will never again complain to the police."

THE STRANGE PERSONALITY OF ADOLF HITLER

THE DOMINANT FIGURE IN GERMAN NAZISM

Adolf Hitler, born into a middle-class Austrian family, was the dominant force in nazism, his beliefs forever linked with its history. He was a failure at school and was usually jobless. His only success was in building the Nazi party and leading it to victory in Germany.

It is possible to call Hitler insane and a genius in the same sentence. A man of strange contradictions, he was shy, retiring, and a loner—and a leader of enormous force. Passionately single-minded, he rarely changed his mind about anything. He was a brilliant orator, though he was coarse, repetitious, and unclear on issues.

THE PUBLIC AND PRIVATE MAN

Hitler often dwelled in a fantasy world. He enjoyed children's adventure books, hated to go to bed, and loved to ride in fast cars. He dreamed about heroic Germans who would change the world.

He spent his early years unemployed and in poverty, yet said, "But in my imagination I dwelled in palaces." He was slight, unhealthy, and suffered from insomnia, stomach disorders, and anxiety—yet claimed Germans were descended from powerful Teutons and Aryans superior to other people. He did not eat meat or smoke.

WAS HITLER INSANE?

This is a difficult question. According to his own words, he was without conscience. He called conscience "a Jewish invention."

Often his actions were strange. He rarely listened to others and shouted down opponents. He did not engage in normal conversation and even in small gatherings lectured and yelled. He flew into rages with experts who disagreed with him. He claimed to know more about politics than anyone else and more about military tactics than his generals.

Germans followed his lead, sane or insane, and placed him in power. Then they followed him loyally into a war that devastated Germany and a good deal of Europe.

[36]

Photographed
at an unguarded
moment, Hitler
waits to address
a Nazi meeting
at Munich.

Flanked by his
aides, Hitler
marches toward
shaping a new
Germany.

Top: Herman Göring and Hitler meet at the 1938 Nuremberg Rally. Middle: Rudolf Hess and Hitler shake hands. Until Hess flew to Scotland in 1941 the two were almost inseparable. Bottom: the Nazi elite, Hitler, Goebbels, and Göring, gather to watch the 1936 Olympics.

HERMANN GÖRING

The second most powerful man in Germany after Adolf Hitler was Hermann Göring. A robust man who had served as a pilot during the war and been decorated with the nation's highest military medal, Göring became addicted to morphine.

Göring had a certain charm and sense of fun, unlike other Nazi leaders. He had a liking for uniforms, medals, art, and women. Yet ruthlessness marked his career: he created the Gestapo (secret police), the concentration camps, and the Luftwaffe (air force). As the Third Reich marched through Europe, he had captured art works sent to his own home.

Göring became the highest-ranking Nazi captured by the Allies at the war's end. He was tried, found guilty, and sentenced to death for war crimes. But Göring fooled everyone. Two hours before his execution he took poison and died in his cell.

RUDOLF HESS

Twice wounded in the First World War, Hess became a loyal aid to Hitler in the early days of the Nazi movement. When Hitler was sent to prison in 1923, Hess voluntarily joined him to take the dictation for *Mein Kampf*.

Hess believed Hitler almost a god and introduced him to mass rallies as the savior of the Fatherland. Then, in May 1941, on the eve of the German invasion of the USSR, Hess flew a Messerschmitt to Britain and parachuted into Scotland. Hitler denounced him, but many believed he came to arrange a united front of Britain and Germany against the USSR.

After the war, Hess was convicted of war crimes and imprisoned in Spandau prison. By 1978 he was its only inmate.

JOSEPH GOEBBELS

This thin, small man with an unyielding hatred of intellectuals and Jews directed the Ministry of Propaganda. His word was law on what Germans could read, see, or hear.

He was a brilliant speaker, able to spellbind audiences with his clever phrases. He was also obsessed with notions of Aryan superiority and spoke murderous venom toward minorities. He and his entire family died with Hitler in the Berlin bunker in 1945 as Allied forces closed in.

EVERYDAY LIFE IN THE THIRD REICH

GAINING CITIZEN APPROVAL

To win public approval, the Nazis knew they had to do more than silence enemies. They carefully courted the general population with jobs and promises. Although trade unions disappeared, so did unemployment. In five years, production rose by 100 percent, largely through war orders, and Germany became a beehive of activity.

For those who conformed—the majority of citizens—life improved under the Nazis. William L. Shirer, an American reporter, wrote of the average German's response to the New Order: "Somehow it imbued them with a hope and a new confidence and an astonishing faith in the future of their country."

Driving Jews and political foes out of good jobs, homes, and opportunities left more for other Germans. Some were delighted to seize the possessions of those taken off to concentration camps.

COURTING POPULARITY

Nazi slogans sought to win citizen effort for distant goals. "The common interest before the self-interest" was a patriotic slogan. Propaganda Minister Joseph Goebbels put it more accurately another time to an audience: "You are nothing, the nation is everything."

The emphasis on the glories of German history, culture, and virtues impressed many. Hitler promised a new "people's car"—the *Volkswagen*—at a price all could afford. New roads were built, but the Volkswagen never appeared, only military vehicles, for the Third Reich was heading toward war.

A German Work Front told citizens where to work and at what wages. As wages fell, the Work Front offered a program of "Strength Through Joy"—vacations, picnics, concerts, and holiday trips for workers. In 1937 it sent nine and a half million Germans on hikes, trips, and vacations and to plays and concerts.

Through the
celebration of spe-
cial events or holidays,
as in this Hamelin Thanks-
giving Day Harvest (above) and
this "Party Day of Freedom," or Feast
Day, on September 11, 1935, at Nuremberg
(below), Nazis massed their power to win citizen approval.

Above, left: for the German people, Adolf Hitler announced the introduction of the Volkswagen at this ceremony on May 26, 1938. Above, right: parades were a time for demonstrating loyalty, so few turned to look at the camera. Opposite: nazism carefully involved civilians in its military displays.

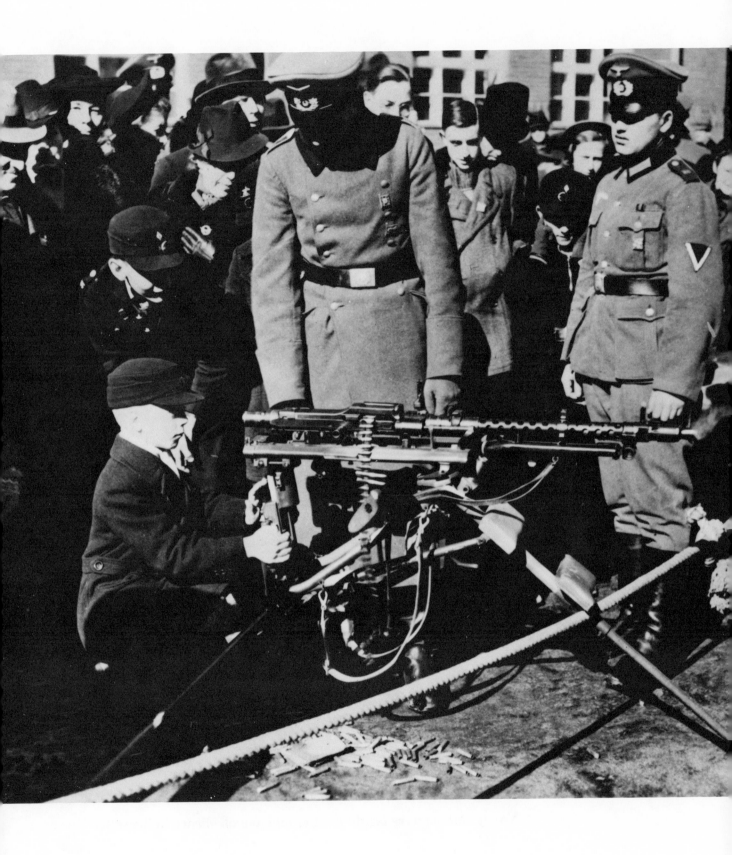

Young and old were taught to offer undying obedience to the state.

ALIGNMENT AND THE MILITARY STATE

GLEICHSCHALTUNG (ALIGNMENT)

Conformity of citizens and their organizations to Nazi goals was carefully supervised. All groups required Nazi approval and leaders. Social, athletic, and professional organizations had to swear undying loyalty to the Third Reich. In 1933 the Mathematical Association wrote:

> ... *We wish thus to conform to the spirit of the total state, and to cooperate loyally and honestly. Unconditionally and joyfully, we place ourselves ... at the service of the National Socialist movement and behind its leader, our Chancellor, Adolf Hitler.*

The Reichstag was ruled by Nazi decree, its meetings powerless to change laws. It was only a short step from alignment to military dictatorship.

THE MILITARY STATE

The Nazis extolled the heroic and military qualities in German culture. Soldiers were treated as heroes, and officers as beyond criticism. Children were taught to admire the military life and those who offered military service to the government.

On the streets of Germany, soldiers helped children, teen-agers and elderly women onto their tanks. Civilians were encouraged to handle the mounted guns on tanks. Parades were special occasions, and families were urged to contribute sons to the German Army.

The militaristic view was further advanced by persecution of minorities and enemies. Citizens were taught to accept brutal and military solutions to peacetime problems. Reporting disloyalty to authorities was encouraged, even children telling of disloyal remarks by their parents and relatives. The state came first in the lives of all.

For those Germans offended by this turn of events, there was the constant threat of arrest and imprisonment. Anyone might report a suspicious remark, and soon the Gestapo would arrive at one's home.

LAW AND JUSTICE IN THE THIRD REICH

THE NAZI LEGAL SYSTEM

The judicial system of Germany conformed to Nazi wishes and political needs. Nazi judges replaced any unwilling to carry out orders from der Führer. Special "people's courts" were established to try treason cases. Scant attention was given to evidence, and there was no appeal to the usual sentence of death.

Nazi officials could intervene in any trial and reverse court rulings. When Pastor Niemöller was acquitted by a court, high Nazi officials had him arrested and sent to a concentration camp anyway. Germany's leading authority on public law, Carl Schmitt, stated, "All law emanates from der Führer."

A vast secret police aided by thousands of informers kept the government informed about the actions and thoughts of citizens. The Gestapo under Heinrich Himmler and another secret police unit under Reinhard Heydrich spied on citizens (including Nazis), staged night raids, tortured their prisoners, and ran the concentration camps. Men and women were jailed without trial or executed at will.

"THE BLOOD PURGE"

On June 30, 1934, Germany saw the Nazi legal system in full view. The Nazis wanted to make peace with army officers, many of whom feared and resented the storm troopers of Ernst Röhm. Under Hitler's orders, a special secret police unit rounded up and massacred leading SA officers. Forgotten was the crucial part that Röhm's roving bands of storm troopers had played in bringing the Nazis to victories at the polls.

The "Blood Purge" of Röhm and his men cemented the alliance between the Nazi state and the army officers. From that point, officers took an oath, a "sacred oath," not to their country or its constitution, but to der Führer.

The massacre of the SA leaders also helped shape a new instrument of terror, the Gestapo. Under the quiet, scholarly-looking Himmler, it became the most feared secret police in history, a law unto itself.

Above: the massacre of storm trooper leaders in 1934 made the German Army supreme, ensured its loyalty to the Nazis, and made it a partner in corrupting justice to suit Nazi ends. Right: the accused had no rights under Nazi law, and justice rested on the whim of Nazi judges or leaders.

**Use of propaganda during the 1936 Olympics in Germany
was designed to win admiration from friend and foe.**

GOVERNMENT BY PROPAGANDA

MASTERS OF PERSUASION

Friend and foe agreed that the Nazis were masters of persuasion. Their threat of force hung over every German. But they also mounted a successful propaganda campaign to win citizens to their aims. People were taught to accept a dictatorship, surrender their will to the state, and accept violence and war as patriotism.

The Ministry of Propaganda under Dr. Joseph Goebbels told each German what to think and believe. None but approved views appeared in books, plays, films, magazines, speeches, or on the radio. Said Hitler, "We have put a stop to the idea that it is part of everybody's civil rights to say whatever he pleases."

"Propaganda must not engage in an objective search for the truth," explained Hitler, for that "might equally serve the other side." When Nazi wartime defeats mounted, the home front heard nothing but good news from the fighting fronts.

THE MASS RALLY

Each autumn a high point of propaganda was reached at the Nuremberg rallies. A striking display of armed might, fireworks, marchers, dazzling night lights, and unfurled banners convinced the hundred thousand enthusiasts of the omnipotence of Nazi might.

Speech after speech by Nazi leaders extolled their glory, rejoiced in the nation's strength, and castigated their enemies. Finally, as tension built up, Hitler was introduced and delivered an emotional outpouring that brought a crescendo of applause.

Despite their irrationality, mass rallies were effective in convincing citizens that their government was correct and should be followed to the death. An entire generation of Germans was educated by this manipulation of their emotions, and then led to do the bidding of the state.

CONTROL OF THE YOUNG

A POWERFUL YOUTH MOVEMENT

In 1933 Germany boasted the most vital Youth Movement in the world. After coming to power, the Nazis sent fifty members of the Hitler Youth to seize the German Youth Association building and funds. By 1936 the Catholic Youth Association and all others were banned.

Baldur von Schirach, Youth Leader of the Nazi party, organized young people to serve the state. Until age nine, youths were enrolled in the Hitler Youth. At ten, boys joined the Young Folk and swore obedience to "the savior of our country, Adolf Hitler." From fourteen to eighteen they belonged to the regular Hitler Youth. At eighteen they entered the Work Service and then the German Army.

Throughout their lives, in school and out, young men and women were educated to "serve the nation and the racial community." Children were asked to spy on their relatives and friends and report any disloyalty. But youth training also built up the health, strength, and enthusiasm of the participants and provided work and purpose for the unemployed.

EDUCATION AND RACE

Young men and women were indoctrinated in the Nazi theory that race determined everything—intelligence, personality, and national survival. Bernhard Rust, an SA officer once dismissed as a schoolteacher for mental instability, was in charge of Nazi education. Teachers were compelled to take a loyalty oath to nazism, teach racial doctrines, and serve in a Nazi organization.

Nazi racial ideas ruined education. Racial science and engineering turned out to be poor science and engineering. Education courses in technology and science lost half their students, yet the emphasis continued. In 1938 Philipp Lenard, winner of the 1905 Nobel Prize in Physics, wrote: "science—like anything else created by man—is conditioned by blood and race. . . . People of different racial mixtures have different ways of pursuing science. The Jew is remarkably lacking in a feeling for truth."

Physical endurance was stressed in schools and youth groups. In this and its racial teaching, nazism was training the young to accept racism and war and surrender their minds to the state.

Above, left: in German education and leisure activities, great emphasis was placed on building physical health and stamina among the young. Above, right: Baldur von Schirach directed the Hitler Youth groups. Right: Nazis seized and rebuilt the German Youth movement.

Above: a procession of Nazi art passes before leaders of the Third Reich. Right: Hitler and Goebbels at the German Art exhibit at Munich. Below: the first step in control of culture was gathering up books that disputed Nazi aims or were written by untermenschen.

THE MANIPULATION OF CULTURE

THE REICH CHAMBER OF CULTURE

Under the Ministry of Propaganda, Dr. Joseph Goebbels controlled cultural expression in Germany. He sought to unify all creative talent behind support for the state.

Special departments of his Reich Chamber of Culture regulated art, music, literature, the press, radio, and films. Said Goebbels: "The Reich must not only determine the lines of progress, mental and spiritual, but also lead and organize the professions." Nazi party members controlled professional organizations and gained job preference.

IMPACT ON GERMAN CULTURE

Before 1933 German culture was considered among the greatest in the world. Nazism wrecked that. In 1937 Hitler personally selected 900 works of "great Aryan art" exhibited in Munich. U.S. reporter William L. Shirer found the display "the worst junk this writer has ever seen." Fewer than half a million people toured the exhibit. When Nazis displayed pieces of "decadent art," two million Germans flocked to the exhibit. The government hastily closed it.

Books, radio, magazines, plays, and films echoed the Nazi themes. The result was dull, repetitous, and silly. There was praise for the family, high birth rates, and Nazi leaders. There was condemnation of bachelors, Jews, and "enemies of the state."

The population reacted to cultural propaganda by attending grade-B American films, complaining about the dullness of radio programs, and objecting to the repetition of Nazi virtues in magazines and newspapers. About a third of the newspapers had to close for lack of readers.

But efforts to shape thought control and persuade citizens of their patriotic duty toward the Third Reich did succeed. The overwhelming majority of Germans supported the Nazi plan and were prepared to defend it with their lives.

FROM MYTH TO POLICY

Nazi thinking was dominated by strange and unscientific ideas about race. Germans, according to these, were superior beings, and Jews, Slavs, and Gypsies were *Untermenschen*—dangerous or worthless people. Germans should rule the world and *Untermenschen* should be destroyed.

Under the code name Aktion T4, the Third Reich began its effort to eliminate *Untermenschen*. Those hospitalized for mental or physical illnesses were selected for death by doctors. Many died at the hands of their doctors.

But Aktion T4 was only a first step against the *Untermenschen*. The Nazis moved to escalate traditional European anti-Semitism into a war against its Jews. The war became a major Nazi effort, equal in size to the invasion of a foreign nation.

THE NUREMBERG LAWS

The Nazi war against the Jews began in the streets of the Weimar Republic. In 1935 the annual Nazi rally at Nuremberg passed laws that denied citizenship to Jews and encouraged police and citizen brutality toward Jewish people.

By 1939 some of Germany's Jews were forced to wear a yellow Star of David over their hearts when in public. Jews could not marry or even associate with Christian women. They could not display their war medals or the German flag.

THE NIGHT OF BROKEN GLASS

In 1938 the Nazis carried out a major test of their anti-Semitic campaign. In one November night 195 synagogues were burned, more than 7,500 Jewish shops were wrecked, and men, women, and children lost their lives. So many windows were smashed that it was called "the night of broken glass." The Jews were taxed to pay for the damages.

By early morning thousands of Jews lined up before the U.S. and British embassies to leave Germany. Nazis attacked the lines. At this time, however, Nazis did not object to Jews fleeing their homeland. Half of Germany's Jewish population escaped.

For the rest a nightmare was on the way—while a world stood by in silence.

Above: a 1933 Nazi sign reads, "Germans Defend Yourselves! Don't Buy in Jewish Shops!" Right: arrested and sent to concentration camps where they were starved, beaten, and sometimes slaughtered were people considered physically or mentally inferior, dangerous, or a nuisance to the government.

Right: Nazis found women useful for propaganda photographs extolling the value of producing children for the Nazi armies. **Below:** women were always pictured as standing by to aid their men. This women's battalion marched at Nuremberg in 1938, 2,000 strong, with some 40,000 men.

THE WOMEN OF THE ARYAN RACE

THE PLACE OF WOMEN

In the eyes of the Nazi party, women belonged in the home, and their only role was that of wives of strong men and mothers of healthy children. The job of women, said Hitler, was to develop "a healthy, manly race."

In assigning women to the home, Nazis claimed they were preventing them from losing to men in the competition of life. They were keeping the family strong and keeping women from entering areas "in which [they] will necessarily be inferior."

Mothers who raised large families were praised and rewarded in the Third Reich. On Mothers' Day 1939 three million women received medals for producing large families. Large families meant more soldiers for the army.

THE ATTACK ON EQUALITY

Nazi doctrine viewed equality of the sexes as "a Communist plot." Women were not permitted to serve in high government offices. Nazi philosopher Alfred Rosenberg said, "Only man must be and remain a judge, soldier and ruler of the state."

Hitler made this more explicit:

If today a female jurist accomplishes ever so much and next door there lives a mother of five, six, seven children, who are all healthy and well-brought-up, then I would like to say: From the standpoint of the eternal value of our people the woman who has given birth to children and raised them and who thereby has given our people life for the future has accomplished more and does more!

During the 1930s, as women gained new rights elsewhere, they lost ground in Germany. Fewer women entered universities and better jobs. "There is no place for the political woman in the ideological world of National Socialism," said a Nazi authority.

Adolf Hitler personally enjoyed the company of attractive women, but they were selected for their lack of intelligence and inability to challenge him.

If nazism enslaved its workers and betrayed its middle class, it delivered the goods to its bankers and industrialists. Unions were smashed and communism destroyed. The Nazi state declared that huge companies were compulsory, and the Ministry of Economics ordered firms to join. Those who had paid for the dictatorship were paid back in full.

Big business thrived under Nazi rule. By 1938 the armament industry had tripled its profits and large corporations scored record gains. However, the real wages of workers—what they could buy with their marks—fell.

Big business became a full partner in the Nazi drive for world domination. The Krupp arms company established factories near concentration camps, and its 100 factories across occupied Europe used 100,000 slave workers. In its plants, men, women, and children were sometimes worked to death.

I. G. Farben manufactured the chemical gas used to slaughter millions. Other companies placed bids to build the gas ovens that burned the bodies. German business reaped profits from death.

THE SMALL BUSINESS The Nazi party won the support of small business people by a promise to halt communism and protect free enterprise. Nazi economic policy virtually ended small business in Germany. In 1937 it dissolved all corporations with capital under a certain amount. To start up, a company had to have enormous capital. A fifth of all firms closed.

Some profited from persecution of Jews and others by taking over their concerns when they went to concentration camps.

Hitler (third from right) courted and later rewarded the military and the rich.

Above left: after hearing a Nazi speech extolling work, these Germans march back to their jobs. Above right: these members of the German stock exchange were pleased with Nazi promises to restore prosperity and smash unions and communism.

THE WORK FRONT The Work Front that replaced free trade unions forbade strikes and dictated wages to workers. Company officers decided what they wished to pay, and the Work Front enforced this decision. Nazi officials informed workers that their employers made all rules and deserved unquestioned loyalty.

The average weekly wage in the Third Reich was very low, with a third going for social security and the government. Workers had to carry workbooks that told of their skills, job history, and residence. They had no freedom of choice in jobs.

Right: Prime Minister Chamberlain of Britain believed that Hitler Germany would be pacified if handed certain European lands. The Nazi appetite only increased with this policy of "appeasement."

Left: Sude-ten Germans welcome the Nazi occupation of their land. Opposite: Soviet and Nazi officials negotiated a pact that permitted Germany to wage war in the West without fear of a Soviet attack on the East.

"TODAY GERMANY, TOMORROW THE WORLD"

REARMING GERMANY

The Nazis had promised to violate the Treaty of Versailles and rearm. In 1935 they announced a rearmament plan. The next year German troops reoccupied the Rhineland and remilitarized it. The world stood by and watched. Conscription for the army began.

New military orders meant many more jobs, pleasing everyone from the wealthy munitions manufacturers and bankers to the average citizen. In the public mind, jobs and war orders were united.

THE NAZI WAR MACHINE

In *Mein Kampf,* Hitler made clear the Nazi philosophy and intentions toward the world: "Those who want to live, let them fight, and those who do not want to fight . . . do not deserve to live." Germany needed *Lebensraum*—living space—and Europe "exists for the people who possess the force to take it."

A powerful Germany began to seize European territory. In 1938 Austria was annexed. Then Germany demanded and took the Sudetenland, a part of Czechoslovakia with a large German population. Within six months it seized all of Czechoslovakia. Britain, America, France, and the USSR stood by.

Opposite: nazism brought destruction to Europe and left a grisly heritage. Right: Nazi forces rolled across Europe.

Emboldened by its striking victories without firing a shot, the Nazi war machine became more ambitious. It divided allies by playing on their fear of communism and Soviet Russia, and compelling nations to "appease" the Nazi appetite for land. Hitler was able to demonstrate Nazi daring and expose his divided and weak opponents.

THE SECOND WORLD WAR

In 1939 German Panzer (tank) divisions and Stuka dive-bombers invaded Poland. This time Britain and France declared war. But German armies slashed through Europe in a *blitzkreig,* or lightning war.

Nazi regiments crushed Poland, Denmark, and Norway and marched into France. In forty-three days, French resistance collapsed. In June 1941 Germany attacked the USSR, and at the end of the year Japan attacked the United States. The world was in flames, reeling from the blitzkreig.

By 1942 the swastika flew over most of Europe.

THE SWASTIKA FLIES OVER EUROPE

CARRYING THE ARYAN DOCTRINE TO EUROPE

In the wake of Nazi advances, special Gestapo units began to round up and murder Jews and Communists. People were shot, strangled, hanged, burned, buried alive, or hacked to death with axes. Participating were local anti-Semitic groups from many European nations.

Racial doctrines now covered other nations. Said Nazi Martin Bormann:

The Slavs are to work for us. In so far as we don't need them, they may die. . . . As for food they won't get any more than is absolutely necessary. We are the masters. We come first.

The Aryan creed fitted into the Nazi plan to eliminate leaders of subjugated nations. Hitler announced, "All representatives of the Polish intelligentsia are to be exterminated." Captured nations were given small food supplies, less medical care, and vicious treatment. Heinrich Himmler, Gestapo chief, said, "What happens to a Russian, to a Czech does not interest me in the slightest."

THE RAPE OF EUROPE

Nazi rule in captured nations rested on brute force, and anything of value was shipped to Germany. Göring wrote his subordinates:

Whenever you come across anything that may be needed by the German people, you must be after it like a bloodhound. It must be taken out . . . and brought to Germany.

About 7,500,000 Europeans became forced workers for the Nazis. Overworked men, women, and children, including captured soldiers, died by the thousands. They were poorly fed, badly treated, and sometimes slain by their captors.

By keeping people underfed and weak, the Nazis planned to make revolt impossible. But Nazi oppression spawned a resistance movement and workers in conquered nations sabotaged the German war effort.

Nazi troops execute a French partisan; the partisans were part of the resistance movement.

When Nazis marched off residents of the Warsaw Ghetto, resistance
broke out, led by young people with homemade and stolen weapons.

"THE FINAL SOLUTION OF THE JEWISH QUESTION"

FROM GHETTO TO SLAUGHTER

As Nazi armies rolled across Europe, Jews not massacred by the Gestapo were herded into ghettos. Registered, watched, and slowly starved, the Jews felt the worst had come to pass. They were wrong.

On December 8, 1941, Nazi officials opened a new kind of camp for Jews. Ghetto residents were urged to accept "resettlement" to these work camps. Extra food, gifts for children, and other bribes were offered the bewildered Jews. Every effort was made to mask the real destination.

Squeezed into rail cars, Jews were shipped from all over Europe to Poland. Crowding and little water or food led to many deaths in the cattle cars. But on arrival, armed Gestapo troops—and sometimes marching bands and candy for the children—greeted the arrivals. No sign was given that this was the end of the line, the end of life.

THE DEATH CAMPS

The Jews were examined and healthy ones selected for work battalions. Numbers were tattooed or branded on their skin.

The others were sent into large chambers for "showers." But when huge steel doors closed behind them and Zyklon-B gas was released, they began to scream. Within half an hour the screaming stopped and all were dead. Workers removed gold from the teeth of the dead and carted their bodies off to huge ovens for burning.

Thirty death camps slaughtered six million Jews and two million others, including Gypsies, Poles, and Russians. Few escaped to tell of the holocaust. "Resettlement" of Jews continued for years without Jews discovering their destination was a death camp.

RESISTANCE

Those not put to death immediately tried to resist in each camp. Slave workers tried to manufacture explosives, slay guards, and destroy gas chambers. But they were not armed, and their captors were.

Their resistance drew little outside support. The Polish underground was not helpful, and the Allies refused to bomb the camps or trains that daily brought new murder victims. But resistance continued, a last hopeless assertion of humanity by the doomed.

Even as Germany battled to win the war, some Nazi officials insisted on trains carrying people to death camps rather than carrying troops to where they were needed. The army and Gestapo argued over the destiny of the Third Reich and who should be killed first—enemies or innocents.

Opposite: Jews from all over Europe were rounded up, identified, and kept in ghettoes to await a "final solution." Above, left: in the Warsaw Ghetto, a Jewish death wagon waits to take bodies for burial. Right: an American soldier examines the urns for storing the ashes of concentration camp victims slain and cremated.

BEFORE GERMANY

The Wallachs were a Jewish family that traced its roots to the soil of Bohemia before the birth of the German nation. Starting around 1570, they produced doctors, merchants, craftsmen, lawyers, soldiers, and public officials.

They were generally upper-middle-class people, respectable members of their communities. In their beloved homeland they found social, financial, and personal rewards.

NAZISM DISCOVERS THE WALLACHS

Nazism was born in Munich, home of the Wallachs. During the 1923 Munich Beer Hall Putsch, Moritz Wallach was held as a hostage by the Nazis. By the time nazism came to power the Wallach Museum of Folk Art was famous. It was dedicated to preserving German national folk art. Its products reached into many homes, including that of der Führer.

Repeatedly the Wallachs resisted the Nazi effort to humiliate them and destroy their standing in the community. When swastikas were painted over their shop windows, they offered a display in the small clear spots. They refused to sell their business to a Nazi until 1939, when they were forced to.

As the Nazi anti-Semitic attack increased, forty-one Wallachs fled their homeland. The young escaped, but the elderly, thinking they would be safe, remained.

THE HOLOCAUST Fourteen Wallachs—one-fourth of the family—did not survive. One elderly Wallach, living in The Hague, turned himself in to the Gestapo in 1942. He did not believe they "would harm an old gentleman." In forty-eight hours he was on his way to Auschwitz and death.

One Wallach lived out the war safely married to an "Aryan." Another fought in the Dutch resistance. Another couple escaped when a Nazi diplomat used them as a cover for his trip to Manchuria. After the "night of broken glass," several gained admittance to the United States.

Their loyalty to the Fatherland, their wealth and intelligence, did not save the Wallachs from the Nazi onslaught. But this Jewish family was luckier than most. Their incredible story is told by a relative, Catherine Hanf Noren, in *The Camera of My Family* (New York: Knopf, 1976).

Opposite: the Wallachs, like other Germans, loved hiking and the vigorous life. Adolph (right) died in a concentration camp, two others died before, and two others survived the holocaust. Left: against a background of fabrics designed by the Wallachs, der Führer enjoys a moment during a holiday.

EUROPE COMBATS NAZI RULE

THE MANY FORMS OF BATTLE

Nazi rule never crushed the spirit of opposition. More than a million Germans were sent to concentration camps—testimony to their resistant spirit. Resistance centered in the ministry and the military. In the army a group led by an officer named Beck early tried to convince France and England to halt Nazi imperialism. It hoped outside opposition would topple the Nazi leadership.

Resistance mounted during the war and as Nazi oppression became more extensive and cruel. On July 20, 1944, another group carried out an attempted assassination of der Führer. But after Colonel Claus von Stauffenberg placed a bomb near Hitler during a conference, another officer accidentally moved it. Hitler was unhurt by the blast. The Gestapo arrested 7,000 and executed 5,000 people.

Elsewhere in Europe, opposition took many forms. Denmark's citizens saved virtually all their Jewish citizens from Nazi capture. Their king proudly wore a Jewish armband to show his solidarity with all his people. In Yugoslavia, Marshal Tito led partisan bands that kept Nazi armies on the defensive throughout the war. European slave workers sabotaged goods marked for the German war machine. Partisans from France to the USSR blew up rail bridges and Nazi supplies and communication systems. Gestapo leader Reinhard Heydrich was assassinated by Czech partisans—and in retaliation Nazis destroyed the entire village of Lidice.

Interference in army matters led to an attempted assassination of der Führer in 1944.

Children play in the rubble that was the Warsaw Ghetto.

THE WARSAW GHETTO UPRISING

A dramatic instance of anti-Nazi daring took place in the large Gestapo-controlled Jewish ghetto of Warsaw. As plans were made to remove the last 60,000 to death camps, the Jews fought back. With a few pistols and grenades captured from the enemy and an iron will, they made their stand. Emmanuel Ringelblum wrote of their decision to fight:

> *We took stock of our position and saw this was a struggle between a fly and an elephant. But our national dignity dictated to us that the Jews must offer resistance and not allow themselves to be led wantonly to the slaughter.*

The Gestapo had to call for reinforcements, flamethrowers, and tanks. It took more than four weeks to crush the men, women, and children of the Warsaw ghetto. In the end the ghetto was rubble, death, and flaming resistance.

Above, left: der Führer and Eva Braun at a happy moment. Above, right: youthful Nazi recruits surrender to the U.S. Army that knifed into Germany in 1945. Center: British Field Marshal Montgomery (left) receives the surrender of Germany from Admiral Doenitz and Field Marshal Keitel (with hats) in May 1945.

THE DEATH OF NAZISM IN EUROPE

THE DEFEAT OF GERMANY

In 1933 Nazi leaders proclaimed the "Thousand-Year Reich." But by April 1945 it was over. The New Order lay in shambles, bombs reduced German cities to rubble, and citizens searched for food and relatives.

As allied armies crashed into Berlin, Hitler, who had just married Eva Braun, committed suicide. At Hitler's last order, Martin Bormann burned his body.

The Nazi high command surrendered and the Nazi party collapsed. Its leaders committed suicide, escaped to South America, or were captured by the Allies. The war involved over 60 nations, killed 29,000,000 soldiers and civilians and cost vast sums of money. The agony of World War I had been multiplied many times over in World War II.

THE GERMAN PRICE OF NAZI RULE

For Germany, Nazi rule could be measured in money, lives, and a civilization lost. Of Frankfurt's 177,000 houses, only 44,000 were left standing. In Nuremberg 9 out of 10 houses were destroyed or damaged. Entire families were wiped out, and none was left without grief. So many Germans died fighting for the Third Reich that Allied troops found youths of fifteen in Nazi uniforms. The German Army no longer looked, sang, or marched like a master race.

Nazism had provided jobs—war jobs. It had brought disgrace to an entire nation through its policies of genocide and slavery. It gutted the arts, education, and culture and marched its youth to death. It had ruined the reputation of a great nation and left an everlasting stain.

In replacing a weak republican form of government with a strong totalitarian one, Germans had sealed their fate. They had surrendered their power to a single party and paid the price in blood.

DESTROYING NAZISM: PRELUDE AND INTERRUPTION

THE NUREMBERG TRIALS

At the war's end, the leading Allies were united in their determination to destroy nazism and German militarism forever. Nazi officials were removed and the party banned.

Legal experts from France, Britain, the USSR, and the U.S.A. conducted a spectacular trial of leading Nazis from November 1945 to October 1946. Charged with crimes against world peace, soldiers, civilians, prisoners, and slave workers were twenty-two Nazis, including Hermann Göring.

The defendants claimed they were innocent of all crimes and only followed orders. Some blamed Hitler alone. But evidence established that many had issued orders that led to the death of millions. Three were acquitted. Of the nineteen Nazis found guilty, ten were executed. Other trials followed to punish those who had ordered the death of innocent victims in Germany or in Europe.

Opposite, left: Nazi defendants at the Nuremberg trials listen to testimony against them. Opposite, right: Brigadier General Telford Taylor helped conduct the American prosecution case. Right: the leading defendants, Göring, Hess, and Ribbentrop, at Nuremberg.

THE COLD WAR INTERVENES

Hardly had the proceedings begun against nazism than the "cold war" between the U.S.A. and USSR interrupted. Efforts to remove and punish Nazis slowed down as both sides busied themselves lining up allies.

Germany became a pawn in the cold war, sought by both sides. In both the U.S. and Soviet sectors of Germany, Nazis found their way back into high positions. Both sides claimed that ex-Nazis now aiding them were "cleansed" of nazism. The U.S. High Commissioner for Germany pardoned many convicted war criminals.

Old Nazis gained important posts in West Germany. Hans Globke, who wrote a book to defend the anti-Semitic Nuremberg laws, became Secretary of State and Secretary to Chancellor Adenauer of West Germany. He was received by the Pope and toasted by Soviet Premier Khrushchev. From 1957 to 1964 Theodore Maunz, who defended Gestapo law, was Bavarian Minister of Education. Otto Ambros, who manufactured Zyklon-B gas for I. G. Farben, was placed on several corporation boards of directors.

Removing Nazis became a joke, with each side seeking only to remove the other side's Nazis. To the victims of nazism, however, the West German government tried to make amends by offering aid to the survivors in Germany and Israel.

Right: General Eisenhower (in the middle of the background), shocked at the concentration camps his troops liberated, compelled local Germans to tour them. Thus began the process of facing the terrible past. Below, left: Ilse Koch, wife of the commandant of Buchenwald, was sentenced to life imprisonment for sending men, women, and children to death. Below, right: German boy scouts, as part of a national effort to atone for Nazi crimes, restore a damaged Jewish cemetery in Pfalz.

GERMANY FACES ITS NAZI PAST

A NATIONAL AMBIVALENCE

Germans have made great efforts to face their Nazi past and suffered enormous pain in doing so. In a speech delivered by a young writer for the day Germans remember their war dead, this agony is apparent:

> *How—I ask you and I ask myself—are we to commemorate those who fell in the last two wars? Can we speak of them as of the defenders of Thermopylae who fought to the last man against the barbarian hordes? No, we cannot. It is we ourselves who were the barbarians in the last war.*

The West German government has paid reparations to families of its Nazi victims—and has also provided aid to the families of ex-Nazis. Some Germans insist, "I don't want to hear of Nazis any more!" and others have said, "We must continue to examine why our parents acted as they did."

Perhaps the national division is illustrated in attitudes toward the state of Israel. Some Germans have sided with the Arab cause, while the government of Germany has paid large reparations to Israel and been a fast ally.

THE CHALLENGE TO GERMAN EDUCATION

Only with reluctance have German schools faced the study of the Nazi era. Some history courses end in 1932, and textbooks omit mention of Nazi atrocities, the Gestapo, and sometimes even Hitler and World War II.

Some teachers have fearlessly taught about the horrors of the Third Reich, and others have said this would only create guilt in their students. In 1977 a teacher collected more than 3,042 compositions by teen-agers about Adolf Hitler. Most wrote of an important leader who gained valuable things for his nation.

This teacher concluded that his nation needed far more accurate study of the Nazi era. German education is wrestling with this question.

NAZISM STAGES A COMEBACK IN GERMANY

REVIVAL IN GERMANY

In 1977 a group of students at the Armed Forces University in Munich ended a drinking bout with a symbolic burning of Jews. They scribbled the word *Juden* ("Jews") on pieces of paper, burned them, exchanged Nazi salutes, and sang a Nazi hymn. School officials tried to hush up the incident and, in violation of the regulations, failed to report it to the Defense Minister.

This incident was one of many that demonstrated that nazism was still alive in Germany. In 1976 the Minister of the Interior announced:

> *At no time since the collapse of 1945 has national socialism been glorified so openly in speeches, pamphlets, and activities . . . or the democratic, law-based state been so despised by its opponents.*

A number of books appeared that mocked charges of Nazi atrocities. One was called *The Auschwitz Lie: Did Six Million Really Die?* Another was entitled *Why We Germans Are Lied To*. These publications aided new groups springing up.

Opposite, left: two neo-Nazis, separated in court by an officer, defaced a Cologne synagogue on Christmas Eve, 1959. This incident touched off a chain of worldwide anti-Semitic incidents in 1960. Arnold Strunk (right) told the court Hitler was right on certain matters. Opposite, right: Germans in several cities attended this photograph exhibit showing the wartime murder and persecution of Jews. Left: Spandau prison continued to hold Rudolf Hess and became a focus of neo-Nazis who demanded Hess be freed. Russian and U.S. soldiers alternately guard the prison.

THE NEO-NAZIS

About 120 organizations in Germany draw inspiration from the Nazi era. Their total membership is placed at about 22,000, a drop from 30,000 in 1970. They publish 78 weeklies with a circulation of 197,000. They generally attack the German Republic and Israel, accept race as central to civilization, and assail communism, as did the Nazis.

Beginning in 1975, these groups organized street demonstrations. They shouted Nazi slogans and combined attacks on Israel, communism, and the government with demands for amnesty for convicted Nazi criminals. Some have adopted bombings and other terrorist acts to win attention and victories. They train young people to glorify violence, store weapons, and wait for the right moment. In 1978, a West German official said 900 to 1,000 right-wing terrorists serve in 25 to 30 neo-Nazi groups.

The German government has watched these movements carefully and rarely intervened. Some groups have connections in the United States, where they appear to gain their funds, and in Europe and the Arab countries.

Top, left: in 1960, Israeli agents in Argentina seized Adolf Eichmann, who directed the mass murder of European Jews, and flew him to Jerusalem for trial. Standing in the case of glass on the right, Eichmann faces the court that sentenced him to death as a war criminal. Bottom, left: in 1964 Paul Leo Leider, an Auschwitz survivor, testified about Nazi torture techniques. Above, right: as this photograph abundantly illustrates, nazism was very popular in Germany, and many people participated in the abuse and slayings of the time. Few have been brought to justice.

THE NAZI WAR CRIMINALS AMONG US

HIDDEN AND FORGOTTEN

In 1960 Israeli agents in Argentina captured Adolf Eichmann, who had directed the execution of European Jewry. Eichmann was spirited off to Israel, tried, and executed for mass murder. The sensational kidnapping and trial focused public attention on the crimes of the Nazi era—and the ability of some top Nazis to escape justice.

Today some still live quiet, unobtrusive lives in Europe, North America, or South America. In 1978 about eighty are known to live in the United States.

They live peaceful lives and are accepted by their local communities. One is a retired carpenter in Mineola, Long Island. One was employed as a CIA agent. One is a bishop in Grass Lake, Michigan. Each entered the United States in violation of the immigration laws and is subject to deportation, yet nothing has been done.

THE TOLERATION OF WAR CRIMINALS

U.S. immigration officials have tried to deport only three of the eighty people. In many cases, files have mysteriously disappeared from or been altered in the Immigration Service offices. Powerful friends in the country have offered them protection and prevented their deportation.

To avoid prosecution, war criminals have played on the general fear or hatred of communism. As ex-Nazis, they claim they would be subject to Communist reprisal if they returned to their home countries. Many would be tried by Communist governments.

So a Surfside, California, man charged with murdering 800,000 Yugoslavs for the Nazis remains on his tree-lined street. So does another who conducted medical experiments at Dachau and was hired here to develop space medicine for NASA.

Most will remain living peacefully in the United States, despite outbursts of public outrage.

THE LESSONS AND FASCINATION OF NAZISM

THE HITLER WAVE

In 1978 people all over the world were caught up in a "Hitler wave." Collectors paid high prices for Nazi emblems, uniforms, and swastikas. Some people considered it fun to wear these relics of the Nazi era.

There was also a growing serious interest in the story of nazism, Hitler's personality, and the causes of World War II. A host of books, documentaries, and films examined this crucial period for humankind. An increase in unemployment and inflation throughout the world reminded people that conditions could again produce nazism.

THE POWER AND THE FURY

In 1945 the U.S. prosecutor at the Nuremberg war trials was Supreme Court Justice Robert Jackson. He told the court:

The wrongs we seek to condemn and punish have been so calculated, so malignant and so devastating, that civilization cannot tolerate their being ignored because it cannot survive their being repeated.

That lesson is still true. Only a study of the nature and tactics of nazism can alert people to the danger of neo-Nazis. The price of liberty is still vigilance.

Those who ignore warnings and proceed without knowledge may lose their freedom.

CAN NAZISM SUCCEED?

Along with the rise of neo-Nazi groups worldwide, there has been a sharp increase of inflation, unemployment, and cynicism about government. Many youths are drawn into religious cults the way they were drawn to Nazi youth groups in Germany.

Can this reservoir of youthful energy, aggravated by unemployment, lead to a Nazi state somewhere? No one can say. The rising activities of neo-Nazis show they think their time has come again.

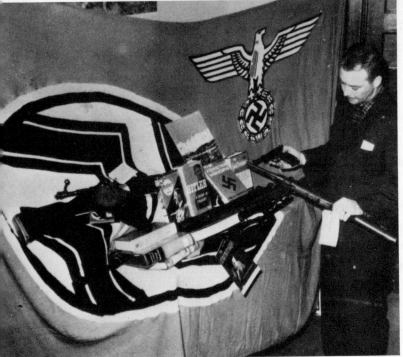

Above, left: the first "Hitler wave," or fad, began when soldiers brought back captured Nazi insignias, hats, and uniforms for their children. Above, right: during the Vietnam War these U.S. neo-Nazis spoke at the Capitol for patriotic support for the war. Left: these neo-Nazi pamphlets and arms were captured in the United States.
Like the Nazis, the neo-Nazis believe in both propaganda and guns.

Above, left: American Nazi leader George Lincoln Rockwell carries a can of gas and matches. He offered to burn those demonstrating in Washington for peace and against the Vietnam War. **Above, right:** these prisoners of the Buchenwald concentration camp were photographed by the U.S. Army on April 23, 1945, to remind the world of war crimes.

A LEGACY THAT NEVER DIED

INTERNATIONAL CONNECTIONS

From Berlin to Johannesburg, from San Francisco to Munich and many places in between, Nazis are active again. In 1976 a Nuremberg march for an SS colonel brought out 800 black-shirted Germans to celebrate the "night of broken glass." In 1978 the American Nazi party planned a march through the Jewish area of Skokie, Illinois, to celebrate Hitler's birthday. Most of the money to support nazism in the world comes from the United States. But the movement has attracted very few women to its marches and demonstrations—and not too many men.

Since the 1930s the American Nazis and the Ku Klux Klan have kept loose working arrangements. Both are dedicated to fighting against communism and for "white rule." The Klan *Crusader* publishes articles by leading German Nazis.

THE VICTIMS LIVE ON ALSO

Another part of the Nazi story has never died—the impact on its victims. Those who survived its horrors cannot forget.

Felicia, aged sixty-nine, spent four years in a concentration camp and has incurable depressions. Franz, aged fifty-two, has woken up screaming every night since his liberation in 1945. His wife has placed an American flag at the foot of his bed so that, upon waking, he can see he is safe. Moshe, aged sixty-one, was forced to cart dead bodies from the gas chambers to the crematoria. Every day he takes five showers and changes his clothes three times.

These survivors are also spread out across the world—from Israel to Illinois. Even their children are affected. Though born in freedom, the children of these victims often show severe personal problems. A Nazi era they never knew is still with them.

Alan Bullock. *Hitler: A Study in Tyranny*. New York: Harper and Row, 1962.

Lucy S. Dawidowicz. *The War Against the Jews*. New York: Holt, Rinehart and Winston, 1975.

Henry Gilfond. *The Reichstag Fire*. New York: Franklin Watts, 1973.

Raul Hilberg, ed. *Documents of Destruction*. Chicago: Quadrangle, 1971.

Milton Meltzer, ed. *Never to Forget: The Jews of the Holocaust*. New York: Harper and Row, 1976.

George L. Mosse, ed. *Nazi Culture*. New York: Grosset and Dunlap, 1966.

Ernst Nolte. *The Three Faces of Fascism*. New York: Holt, Rinehart and Winston, 1965, 1966.

Joachim Remak, ed. *The Nazi Years*. Englewood Cliffs, N.J.: Prentice-Hall, 1969.

William L. Shirer. *The Rise and Fall of the Third Reich*. New York: Simon and Schuster, 1960.

Louis L. Snyder. *Hitler and Nazism*. New York: Franklin Watts, 1961.

David Sumler. *A History of Europe in the Twentieth Century*. Homewood, Ill.: Dorsey Press, 1973.